5 Steps to

Understanding

Cholesterol

Learn about

5 Steps to Understand
Cholesterol

Dr. ANJALI ARORA

A Sterling Paperback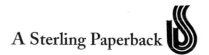

STERLING PAPERBACKS
An imprint of
Sterling Publishers (P) Ltd.
A-59, Okhla Industrial Area, Phase-II,
New Delhi-110020.
Tel: 26387070, 26386209; Fax: 91-11-26383788
E-mail: sterlingpublishers@airtelbroadband.in
ghai@nde.vsnl.net.in
www.sterlingpublishers.com

5 Steps to
Understand Cholesterol

© 2007, *Dr. Anjali Arora*

ISBN 978-81-207-3244-5

The author wishes to thank all academicians, scientists and writers
who have been a source of inspiration.

Printed and Published by Sterling Publishers Pvt. Ltd.,
New Delhi-110020.

Contents

$\mathcal{C}$holesterol is a white, waxy, chemical substance. It is very important for the functioning of every cell of your body. Cholesterol also helps manufacture vitamin D, hormones like cortisol and your sex hormones.

When cholesterol in your body, goes up beyond desirable levels, it can put you at the risk of having a stroke, developing heart disease or other cardiovascular diseases.

1 Test Yourself for Cholesterol

Yes No Diet

☐ ☐ You often eat fried foods or foods high in cholesterol, such as cheese, butter or eggs.

☐ ☐ You eat your food with gravy or sauces regularly.

☐ ☐ You eat rich meat preparations.

Yes No Addictions

☐ ☐ You are a smoker.

☐ ☐ You are unable to quit smoking.

☐ ☐ You chew tobacco.

Lifestyle

Yes	No	
☐	☐	You are overweight and eat plenty of salty foods.
☐	☐	Your blood pressure is higher than 120/80 mmHg.
☐	☐	You exercise less than thrice a week.

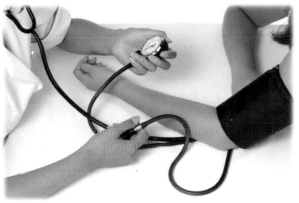

Family History

Yes	No	
☐	☐	You have diabetes or a family history of diabetes.
☐	☐	Your parent/sibling has had a heart attack or stroke or has developed diabetes by the age of 50.

Yes	No	Other Risk Factors
☐	☐	You are a woman on birth control pills nearing menopause.
☐	☐	You drink more than two cups of coffee a day.
☐	☐	You consume a large amount of alcohol every day.

The more times you answer "yes" to the above statements, the greater is your risk of having high cholesterol, coronary heart disease or a stroke.

Cholesterol is manufactured in the body and is also ingested through food like butter, egg yolk and meats. The liver makes most of the body's cholesterol, which helps carry fat to parts of the body that need fat for energy, or storage, such as the hip or belly.

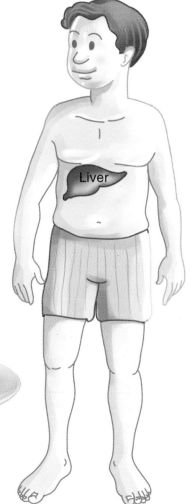

Types of Cholesterol

The liver places cholesterol into packages called lipoproteins made from lipids (fat and cholesterol) and protein. These are of different types.

- LDL-C: Low-density lipoprotein or bad cholesterol
- HDL-C: High-density lipoprotein or good cholesterol
- VLDL-C: Very low-density lipoprotein cholesterol
- Triglycerides: A type of ingested fat
- Lp(a): The worst kind of cholesterol

LDL Cholesterol

It transports cholesterol from the liver to all the cells in the body. If the cholesterol available is more than required, then LDL will end up circulating in the bloodstream and eventually get deposited on the inner walls of the artery. It is called the 'bad cholesterol' because it can cause blockage and result in lack of blood supply.

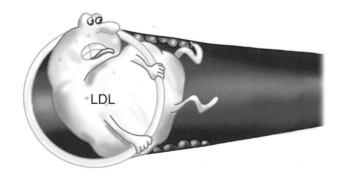

HDL Cholesterol

HDL cholesterol is also known as the 'good cholesterol', as it travels in the bloodstream from the peripheral areas of the body, bringing cholesterol to the liver for break down.

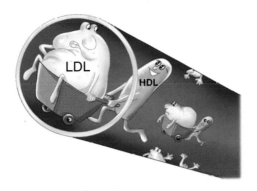

VLDL Cholesterol

Large fat particles called chylomicrons and fatty acids form VLDL. It is used for energy and fat deposition.

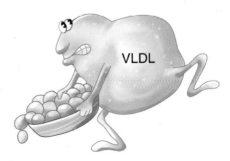

Triglycerides

They are a type of fat also produced by the liver. In human nutrition, more than 95% of the ingested fat is in the form of triglycerides.

Lipoprotein (a)

Over the past few years researchers have identified another form of fat called lipoprotein(a) or Lp(a). It is known to be associated with atherosclerosis and coronary artery disease.

Lp(a) has more to do with genes than diet. Its screening is important to find out an individual's genetic probability of getting heart disease and to help reduce other risk factors which may lead to heart disease.

A high fat diet has been associated with increased incidence of atherosclerosis and coronary artery disease (CAD), obesity and certain cancers.

3 What Does Cholesterol Do?

Cholesterol helps carry digested fat from the liver to the whole body. The blood vessels act as a highway. After fulfilling this function, cholesterol returns to the liver and repeats the process all over again.

1. After fat or food is eaten, it goes through the stomach and is then digested and absorbed in the small intestine. After this it is sent to the liver to be processed and shipped throughout the body.

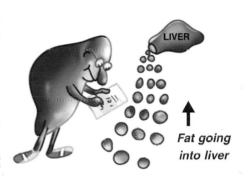

Fat going into liver

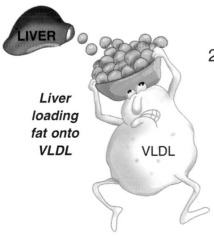

Liver loading fat onto VLDL

VLDL

2. The liver loads the fat on to the VLDLs. These travel through the blood vessels, unloading fat throughout the body. The empty VLDLs then become LDLs.

3. Some LDL pieces can get stuck along the blood vessel walls, thus narrowing the blood vessels.

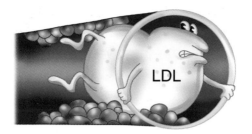

Stuck
LDL

4. The role of HDLs is to separate LDL pieces which are stuck to the blood vessel walls and ship them back to the liver. The LDL pieces are either recycled into new VLDLs or broken down and excreted. The new VLDLs restart the shipment process.

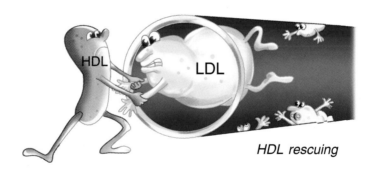

HDL rescuing

When one eats extra fat, more LDL pieces can get stuck along the blood vessel walls, if there are not enough HDLs to release them. Blood vessels can thus get blocked, resulting in a heart attack. Ideally one should have more HDL.

Facts about Atherosclerosis

Atherosclerosis sets in over the years. It can lead to disability and even death. The name *atherosclerosis* is derived from Greek. It refers to the thickening of the arteries over a period of time due to the accumulation of lipids.

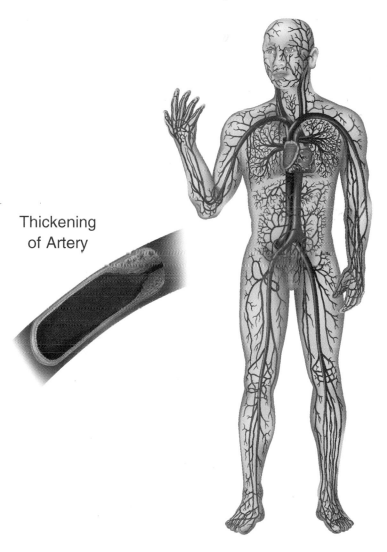

Thickening
of Artery

LDL Oxidation

LDL-C is the major cholesterol that mediates the link between serum cholesterol and atherosclerosis. LDL is modified by certain metabolic processes in the body (e.g. oxidation, acetylation, glycosylation) resulting in the formation of a modified atherogenic LDL. The interaction of this LDL with monocytes (type of cells in our blood) transforms them into foam cells resulting in the formation of atherosclerotic plaques.

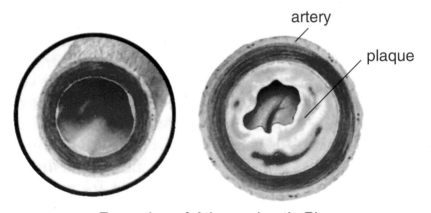

Formation of Atherosclerotic Plaque

Ignored Facts

- High lipids by themselves do not produce any symptoms. It is the pathological involvement with the vessel wall or organ, which leads to the disease process. It is unfortunate that the setting in of hyperlipidemia often goes unnoticed.

Xanthelasma (deposits on the eyelids) and xanthoma (deposition on elbows and other parts of the body) are never taken care of. Many diseases like nephrotic syndrome, atheroemboli of the renal arteries and end-stage renal disease are also the result of high lipids. Pancreatitis can also be a consequence of high triglycerides.

■ Diagnosing atherosclerosis early becomes difficult as there are usually no symptoms, until it is at a fairly advanced stage.

■ Atherosclerosis can be prevented. Its progression can also be slowed by eliminating the factors causing it.

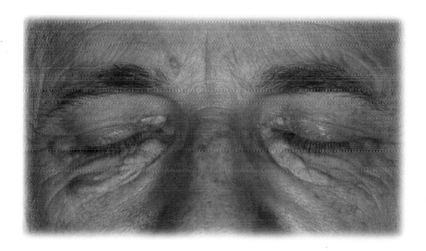

Xanthelasma

A simple blood test gives your total cholesterol and other lipid (fat) levels. Compare your test result with the guidelines below to determine your risk factors. A blood test requiring a 12-hour fast will measure LDL, HDL, VLDL, triglycerides and Lp(a).

Tuberoeruptive xanthomata

Cholesterol Guidelines

Average risk	Borderline high risk	High risk	Goal level	Current risk
200 mg/dl	200-239 mg/dl	240 mg/dl	Under 170 mg/dl	

Other Lipids	Required Levels	Your Current Level
HDL	Men - more than 40 mg/dl Women - more than 50 mg/dl	
LDL	Less than 100 mg/dl	
Triglycerides	Less than 140 mg/dl	
VLDL	Less than 29 mg/dl	
Lp(a)	Less than 20 mg/dl	

Anybody with coronary artery disease, stroke, or two or more risk factors should keep their LDL under 70 mg/dl.

Lp(a) – Another important Lipoprotein

- High lipoprotein (a) is associated with a higher incidence of atherosclerotic and heart disease.
- If your Lp(a) is greater than 20 mg/dl, the risk of atherosclerotic disease can double.
- An increased LDL-C along with high Lp(a) steps up your risk for atherosclerotic disease three to five fold.
- Lp(a) denotes a genetic problem.
- Lp(a) cannot be altered through dietary habits.
- Lp(a) can be reduced with the help of niacin.

LDL Receptors

In 1985, Michael Brown and Joseph Goldstein received the Nobel prize in 1985 for their work on LDL receptors and high cholesterol.

Facts Related to LDL Receptors

- Some people are born with a deficiency of LDL receptors.
- People with LDL receptor deficiency try compensating this defect by producing an excess of LDL or "bad cholesterol".

- In people with a stressed, overindulgent and sedentary lifestyle, high LDL-C is produced.
- This self-made lifestyle results in the reduction of LDL receptors. In both hereditary and cases of self-indulgence, the relationship is between reduced LDL receptors and production of high LDL-C in the blood.

Cholesterol and Lifestyle

A Western lifestyle of high stress, fatty food and sedentary lifestyle leads to ...

- An increase in insulin resistance.
- More production of insulin (due to the consumption of fat or simple sugars).
- Deposits of fat on your belly that leads to abdominal obesity.
- More LDL, that sticks to your arteries and causes blockages.

High cholesterol is regarded as one of the most important factors for plaque deposition and hardening of arteries (atherosclerosis). Like the West, with a high consumption of junk food, this problem is now becoming prevalent among the South Asian population also.

Cholesterol and Emotional Stress

- Emotional stress releases the hormones – adrenalin, noradrenalin and cortisol, which counteract insulin reaction.

- A demand for more insulin is the result.
- This insulin resistance, lipid disorder of low HDL, high triglycerides, apple type obesity and premature coronary artery disease is known as the Reaven syndrome.

Lipoprotein Subfraction Testing

It is done to help evaluate your risk of developing coronary artery disease (CAD). Lipoprotein subfraction tests of LDL are done based upon their size, density, and/or electrical charge. Lipoproteins are heterogeneous particles – containing molecules of proteins, cholesterol, triglycerides and phospholipids. As they circulate in the body, various molecules are removed and others are added to create particles of different compositions. Lipoprotein particles are formed that vary from large and fluffy (those with a high proportion of triglycerides) to small and dense (those with a high proportion of protein). Small dense LDL particles are seen to be more atherogenic (more likely to cause atherosclerosis) than light fluffy LDL particles. Researchers think that the presence of small dense LDL could be one of the reasons that some people have heart attacks even though their total and LDL cholesterol are not particularly high.

The number of small, dense LDL and HDL particles a person has is partially genetically determined. This is partially due to gender (males tend to have more small LDL and HDL than females). It is also related to lifestyle and a person's general state of health. Certain diseases and conditions, such as diabetes and hypertension, are associated with increased levels of small dense LDL.

Lipid subfraction test is conducted by giving a fasting sample of blood for testing in the laboratory (the same way as you give for lipid profile assay).

Lipoprotein subfraction testing is not routinely ordered. It offers useful information in assessing risk in patients who have a personal or family history of early heart disease, especially if their total and LDL cholesterol values are not significantly elevated.

Subfraction testing is usually done along with the lipid profile test. Lipoprotein subfraction testing may also be asked for as part of an overall evaluation of cardiac risk when someone has a personal or family history of early Coronary Artery Disease (CAD), especially when they don't have typical cardiac risk factors, such as high cholesterol, high LDL, high triglyceride, low HDL, smoking, obesity, inactivity, diabetes and/or hypertension. Subfractions can be affected by lipid treatment along

Lipid Subfraction Test

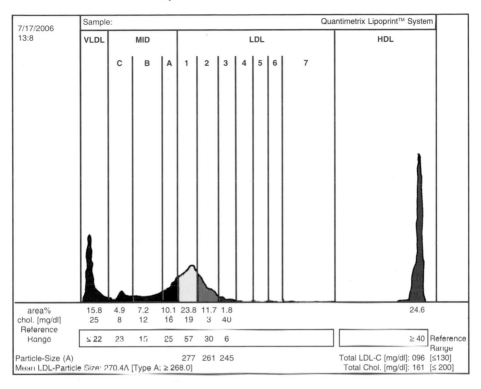

	VLDL	MID			LDL							HDL
		C	B	A	1	2	3	4	5	6	7	
area%	15.8	4.9	7.2	10.1	23.8	11.7	1.8					24.6
chol. [mg/dl]	25	8	12	16	19	3	40					
Reference Range	≤ 22	23	15	25	57	30	6					≥ 40

Sample: 7/17/2006 13:8

Quantimetrix Lipoprint™ System

Reference Range

Particle-Size (A) 277 261 245

Mean LDL-Particle Size: 270.4Å [Type A; ≥ 268.0]

Total LDL-C [mg/dl]: 096 [≤130]
Total Chol. [mg/dl]: 161 [≤ 200]

with lifestyle changes. LDL subfraction testing may also be occasionally ordered to monitor the effectiveness of the treatment in decreasing the number of small dense LDL particles.

Although there is a genetic component, lipoprotein subfractions can be altered by adopting a diet low in saturated fats, losing excess weight and exercising regularly. The use of lipid-lowering drugs may also help affect the subfraction distribution.

HDL Cholesterol

The relative importance of HDL-2 and HDL-3 cholesterol as risk factors for ischaemic heart disease (IHD) is still uncertain.

HDL Particles

- The number of HDL particles a person has is partially genetically determined.
- Studies observe that large fluffy HDL particles may provide more cardiac protection than small HDL particles.
- Males have more small HDL and LDL particles than females.
- Subfractions of HDL: HDL2, HDL3 were seen to be inversely associated with the incidence of ischaemic heart disease.

Blood Sugar and Lipids

You can get your blood sugar tested when you give your blood sample for a lipid profile test. A high level of blood sugar, along with high cholesterol, doubles the risk of CAD and atherosclerosis.

Free Radical Formation

In the presence of excessive free radicals, LDL (the bad cholesterol) changes its form to oxidised LDL, which sticks to the walls of the arteries, thus increasing the possibility of the development of atherosclerosis.

Cholesterol Facts

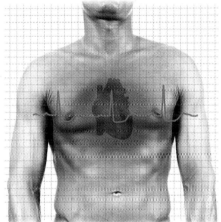

- For every 1% drop in the total cholesterol, there is a 2% decrease in the risk of having a heart attack.
- The risk of heart attack drops by about 4% when HDL levels are increased by 2%.
- The human body manufactures two-thirds of its cholesterol, one-third of which comes in through food.
- Studies state that in most Asian countries, the mean levels of total cholesterol are lower than those found in western countries.
- The incidence of coronary heart disease is also lower, but, incidence of stroke, particularly hemorrhagic stroke, is higher in Asians.

- A clear evidence is present involving hazards of higher systolic blood pressure at all levels of cholesterol and hazards of higher cholesterol diseases at all levels of systolic pressure.
- Effects of major risk factors for cardiovascular disease are considered to be multiplicative.

If 1 factor doubles the risk involved and another triples it, then joint risk factors increase your risk sixfold for cardiovascular disease.

Factors that can affect the blood cholesterol readings are:

- Seasonal variation: Cholesterol is approximately 5% higher in your body in winter than in summer.
- Body weight: On recent loss in weight, your cholesterol is likely to be lower.
- Blood test and body position: Blood test and the position of the body affect levels of blood cholesterol. A change from lying

down to sitting up can raise your cholesterol level. This is due to the presence of increased protein in blood.

Blood Drawing Technique

While drawing a blood sample, if the tourniquet had been tied very tightly or fingers had been squeezed hard, your cholesterol results will show a higher reading. As cholesterol is bonded to blood protein, the extra protein collected will give a high false result due to squeezing.

If your lipid profile report is high you can get it repeated on three different days and compare it. If it remains high, do something about it.

Obesity and High Lipid Levels

Obesity was a common problem in the West, but is now becoming rampant in India and other Eastern countries. Overweight and obese people are commonly known to have high blood cholesterol, high triglycerides and low HDL-C (good cholesterol). Low HDL-C gives them no protection against heart disease.

An increase in LDL-C (bad cholesterol) in obese patients makes them more susceptible to heart problems with excessive amount of calories being taken through saturated fats (*desi ghee*, fried foods and lot of sweets like *khoya barfi*, coconut sweets, chocolates, cakes, etc). Also lack of exercise worsens the situation.

Metabolic Syndrome or Syndrome X

A cluster of risk factors which used to develop with progressive age and post menopause are now seen to develop at 20 and 30 years of age. All over the world (including India) increasing waistlines and potbellies are pointing towards "heart breaking" problems and not prosperity. People developing this syndrome have 2-3 of the following risk factors present.

■ High blood sugar

■ High blood pressure

■ Waist >40 inches in men and >35 inches in women

■ Low HDL-C

■ High Triglycerides

■ Presence of small LDL particles

Metabolic syndrome if not attended to timely, can lead to heart and other associated diseases.

Stress and high levels of cholesterol make a deadly combination for the early development of heart disease.

Women and Cholesterol

Cholesterol levels are seen to increase during pregnancy. During the last trimester (i.e. last weeks of pregnancy), an increase in cholesterol and other lipids is especially seen. This can be attributed to the need for the growing foetus. Also, more fats may be required by the mother during breast feeding.

Menopause

Estrogen is secreted by the female reproductive system until menopause (i.e. 45-50 years of age). Till then, a woman is protected from heart disease as she has a higher HDL and a comparative low LDL. HDL helps clear excessive cholesterol of the body and brings it to the liver for breakdown. This process provides the women

protection against heart disease. As the perimenopausal stage sets in (at about 40-50 years of age), there is a decrease in estrogen production and a reduction in HDL. This makes a woman susceptible to heart disease as much as her male counterpart.

Contraceptive Pills

Oral contraceptive pills are taken by thousands of women around the globe. These pills have been seen to increase cholesterol levels.

Before going on to these hormonal pills, a lipid test must be taken. It is only after your doctor clears you medically, should you start on this medication.

Lipid Disorders in Children

Children under 16 years of age, need to be tested for the detection of any lipid disorder. It is also important to keep a cholesterol baseline record, especially if there is a family history of heart disease or stroke.

Cholesterol Levels in Children

<170 mg/dl	Acceptable
170 – 199 mg/dl	Borderline high
>200 mg/dl	Definitely high

Persistent high levels of cholesterol even in children result in the damage of the blood vessel lining, subsequently leading to build up of atheromatous plaques. Today this can be as a result of sedentary habits (TV and computer watching), consumption of junk food and obesity.

Due to a heavy academic curriculum a child's outdoor activities are restricted. Children who are overweight, have high blood pressure, diabetes or those with a family history of heart disease must get their cholesterol or lipids levels checked.

Monitoring of the blood sugar and lipid profile of school going children should become mandatory. If screening is conducted annually, the cardiac disease process can be nipped in the bud. The percentage of young people developing syndrome X is alarming. Prevention of coronary artery disease must be in the minds of all. Parents of all affected children too should be screened by a physician or at a lipid clinic.

Cholesterol Levels and Older Adults

Coronary disease and high cholesterol levels are seen to develop, more in middle aged people over 50 years and also in older people.

This may be due to less exercise and altering eating habits. Chewing problems with falling teeth and eating out more could also be the reasons. Development of associated diseases like diabetes, blood pressure, arthritis and stress often result in increased cholesterol levels.

HDL-C is also seen to decrease with less exercise. By lowering your cholesterol and other lipids with appropriate medication and lifestyle change, you can add more fruitful years to your life.

Medication Associated with High Cholesterol Levels

Many types of medicines are known to increase cholesterol through their side effects. Some of them are:

Beta Blockers: (Atenolol, Propanolol, Metapropanolol)

Beta blockers are a commonly used medication. One of their main side effects is an increase in LDL cholesterol levels, and a decrease in HDL-C level.

Diuretics: (Hydrochlorthiazide)

These are often given to patients with high blood pressure. Along with the blood pressure medication, patients are advised diuretics to help reduce the fluid load in the body. Diuretics unfortunately not only increase total cholesterol but can decrease the good cholesterol (HDL-C). They also increase the bad cholesterol (LDL-C) and triglycerides.

Some other medication which can derange your cholesterol levels:

- Contraceptive pills
- Corticosteroids (used in rheumatic disease, asthma, etc.)
- Anabolic steroids

Better eating habits, exercising, losing weight, dealing with stress positively and giving up smoking are the quickest ways of developing a healthier lifestyle.

Better Nutrition

A balanced diet helps fight high cholesterol, heart disease, stroke and other related diseases. Good

foods are not manufactured foods. Good foods are natural foods which are nutritious and protect the body against diseases.

Fibre Facts

The indigestible fibre in food is a very important part of healthy eating. It helps in normal bowel movement and lowers cholesterol.

A low-fat, high-fibre diet can help reduce the risk of certain cancers, particularly colon cancer.

Types of Fibre

- Soluble fibre: It swells up and holds water.
- Insoluble fibre: It does not swells up and holds water. It consists of cellulose, the main constituent of cell walls in plants.

Best Sources of Fibre

Soluble Fibre	Insoluble Fibre
Oat bran Oatmeal Beans, peas Lentils Pectin-rich fruits (apples, citrus fruits)	Wheat bran Wheat bran cereal Wholegrain foods (whole wheat, brown rice) Rye bread Vegetables and fruits, if consumed with the skin

A combination of the above will ensure a healthy balance of soluble and insoluble fibre.

Fibre–the Good Cholesterol Lowering Agent

High intake of soluble fibre is known to decrease blood cholesterol by 10-25%. In the western world oat fibre is used regularly. Oats are known to lower absorption of cholesterol in your digestive tract. Isabgol, is an excellent fibre rich product, extensively used in India. It is also known to have excellent cholesterol lowering properties.

Fibre taken through traditional grains and cereals is good for lowering the cholesterol and fats from the body.

Some Beneficial Foods

Garlic: It helps lower cholesterol and prevents hardening of arteries. It also helps in thinning of blood and reduces high blood pressure.

Soya: It contains no saturated fat and can improve good cholesterol levels. It is found in soya oil, tofu and soya milk.

Stanols: They are found in plants and soya bean oil. They help lower cholesterol levels.

Nuts: Almond, walnut and macadamia contain monounsaturated fat, which is good for reducing cholesterol.

Omega Fatty Acids

Omega 3 and Omega 6

They are essential fatty acids which come under special type of polyunsaturated fatty acids.

- Omega 3 fatty acids are found in fish, seafood, nuts like walnut, flax and pumpkin seeds.
- Omega 6 fatty acids are found in sunflower oil, corn and soya bean oils.

Omega 3 Fatty Acids: Are essential fatty acids which are classified under special type of polyunsaturated fatty acids. These fatty acids protect you against heart disease by decreasing the fat and triglyceride levels in your body. They are not made by the body but can be supplied through diet or supplements.

The ability of omega 3 fatty acids to reduce platelet aggregation is important. A diet rich in fish oils and other omega 3 fatty acids also helps reduce clot formation and sticking of the platelets to the arterial walls. This results in less plaque formation and slow development of atherosclerosis.

Niacin: It is a water-soluble vitamin (vitamin B_3) that can lower LDL and increase HDL levels. The best natural sources of niacin are rice bran, wheat bran, peanuts, organ meats like liver and fish like trout, salmon and halibut.

Choose Your Fats Sensibly

Excessive use of fats can increase your cholesterol levels. Fats have more calories (9 per gm) than protein or carbohydrates (4 per gm). To lose weight faster, decrease the fat in your diet.

Monounsaturated Fats: These are present in olive, mustard and rapeseed oils. They are known to increase the levels of HDL (good cholesterol) and lower LDL (bad cholesterol).

Polyunsaturated Fats: They are obtained from safflower, sunflower and corn oil. They can lower your LDL (bad cholesterol), but can also lower your HDL (good cholesterol).

Saturated Fats: Fats from animal sources such as butter, *ghee* and partially hydrogenated oils should be avoided. Fats from vegetable sources like coconut and palm oil are to be used less. Blend two or more oils of different groups. They help in the healthy heart diet. Never reuse fried oil as it is unhealthy.

Reduce the Intake of Cholesterol

Natural foods in balanced and moderate quantities help in cholesterol reduction in a normal healthy adult.

Oil: The quantity of oil and oil products used should not be more than 3-4 teaspoons (in women) and 4-6 teaspoons (in men) daily. The type of oil used is also very important.

Sugar: The quantity of sugar and sugar products used daily should be about 3-4 teaspoons, not more.

Salt: Salt intake should be less than 1 teaspoon daily. This amount of salt (about 1 teaspoon) can be taken in a humid and hot weather.

Fruits: It is a good source of soluble fibre for a normal person. 500 gms of fruits can be taken per day. Reduce the intake of sugar rich fruits like mangoes, grapes and bananas.

Milk: The intake of milk and milk products (of low-fat or skimmed milk) should be about 500 gms per day.

Vegetables: They have negligible calories if not cooked with too much fat. Okra, cucumber, eggplant, cauliflower and french beans are some examples. Some healthy leafy vegetables are lettuce, cabbage, mint, celery, spinach, coriander and soya leaves.

Fish Oils

Fish oils are extracted from fish. Some of them contain polyunsaturated fatty acids that reduce the tendency of blood cells and platelets to form blood clots. They also reduce LDL and triglycerides, and increase HDL.

Fishes which help in lowering cholesterol are usually found in cold ocean waters, for example, salmon.

Eating fish two to three times a week helps in reducing your risk of heart diseases. Taking fish oil capsules can be helpful, but they do not compensate fully for the benefits of actually eating fish.

Labels on canned foods should be read to assess the amount of calories the food contains. Also, avoid foods with preservatives, as excessive salt and colour are harmful to your body.

Some Useful Tips

Dalia (Bulgur Wheat/Bran): Rich in fibre, they bind to cholesterol and fats in the body and helpc in secreting them. Dalia or bran are good as breakfast cereals.

Oats: They contain "Beta glucan" – a soluble fibre. Oat bran helps lower cholesterol levels. It can be mixed in wheat as "atta" or taken as oat rolls or oat porridge.

Esabgol: This rich fibre when taken not only aids in relieving constipation, but helps in eliminating fats and cholesterol from the body. It can be taken before meals or at night after dinner with curd/milk.

Soya and its products: Soya contains antioxidant compounds. It is also known to help blood cholesterol levels. It can be consumed after cooking, as granules or nuggets. Tofu (soya paneer) can be cooked or eaten raw with salad. Soya milk and curd are often substituted for dairy products.

When Buying Dairy Products

■ Milk: Buy fat free milk rather than whole milk or milk with 2% fat. Fat free milk or milk with 1% fat has as much quantity of calcium present as whole milk (Calcium in milk is not related to the fat percentage present).

- Cheese: Look for "fat free", "low fat" or "partly skimmed" cheese. Pick up cheese containing less than 3 gm of fat or less per ounce.
- Soft cheese: Choose the low fat variety.
- Frozen Dairy Desserts: Pick up frozen desserts low in saturated fat. These can be ice milk, low fat frozen yoghurt or fruit juices and sorbets.

- Fats and oils

When Buying Fats and Oils

- Choose liquid vegetable oils like canola, mustard, olive, corn, sunflower and safflower oils.
- Butter, desi ghee and, solid shortenings are rich in saturated fat and cholesterol. These should be consumed in less amount.
- If you need to get margarine, buy it with unsaturated liquid vegetable oils.

When Buying Breakfast Foods

- Choose whole grain breads. They contain more fibre than white bread.

- Eat dry cereals – most of them contain a low fat content.

- Limit the muesli and bran types containing coconut and nuts.
- Avoid sweet baked goodies.
- Low fat sweets and snacks can be eaten once in a while. Remember, these may be low in fat, but not in calories.

American Heart Association

Step I and Step II Diets

Dietary Component	Step I Diet Reversal Diet	Step II Diet
Total fat	30% or less*	30% or less
Saturated fatty acids	8 to 10%	less than 7%
Polyunsaturated fatty acids	up to 10%	up to 10%
Monounsaturated fatty acids	up to 15%	up to 15%
Carbohydrates	55% or more	55% or more
Protein	approximately 15% protein low in fat should be selected	approximately 15% protein low in fat should be selected
Cholesterol	less than 300 mg daily	less than 200 mg daily
Fibre	20 - 30 gms	20 -30 gms
Total calories	to achieve/maintain desired weight	to achieve/maintain desired weight

Percentages refer to per cent of total calories. The reversal diet is a vegetarian diet containing less than 10% total fat and minimal saturated fat.

Proportion of Dietary Components

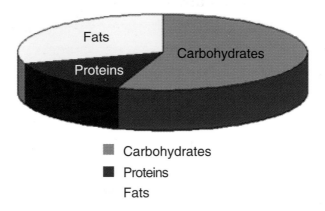

- Carbohydrates
- Proteins
- Fats

Healthy Exercise

It is never too late to get stronger and stay strong.

- Exercise should be done before meals, never immediately after meals.

- If you have a heart problem, hyper-tension or any other special condition, consult your doctor before exercising.

- Listen to your body. When fatigued or unwell, do not exercise.

Exercise should contain three phases: warm-up phase, brisk phase and cool-down phase.

- Exercising during extreme temperatures like very hot or cold weather puts extra burden on your heart and blood vessels.

- When exercising during hot and/or humid weather, decrease the duration and intensity of exercise. Allow your body to warm up and cool down. Drink plenty of water before, during and after exercise.

- In cold weather, avoid heat loss. Dress in layers and remove extra clothing as you warm up.

Watch Your Weight

Your body stores more fat and cholesterol if you are overweight. The fastest way to lose weight is to reduce your intake of fat and sugar.

The Pinch Test

Grasp the skin at the side of your waist between the thumb and the index finger. If it is more than an inch, then you need to lose fat.

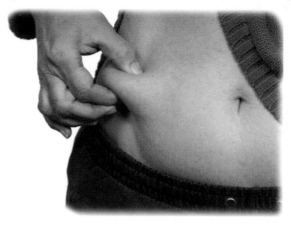

Major effects of lifestyle modification on plasma lipids

Major lipid benefits on intervention due to	Decreased LDL-C	Decreased Triglyceride	Increased HDL-C
Decreased saturated fat	Yes	Yes	
Decreased dietary cholesterol	Yes		
Decreased weight when overweight	Yes	Yes	Yes
Increased physical activity	Yes	Yes	Yes
Cessation of smoking			Yes

De-stressing

Stress is a contributory factor towards high cholesterol levels.

Stress is responsible for excessive secretions of adrenaline and thyroid hormones. It also causes excessive secretion of kidney hormones. Through various mechanisms an increase in cholesterol and blood pressure occurs. Roughening, thickening of the arteries and more fat deposition also takes place. The chances of getting a heart attack or stroke are enhanced.

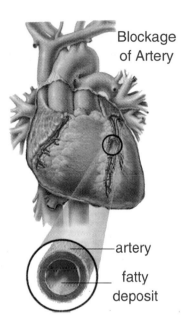

Blockage of Artery

artery

fatty deposit

How to Deal with Stress

- Avoid chronic stress.
- Change your attitude. Situations do not change, you can.
- De-stress yourself.

De-stressing Techniques

Exercise: Desk jobs often involve long working hours at the table or computer. This leads to bad posture, along with chronic stress. One can perform these exercises to help de-stress while working.

- Head rotations
- Shoulder shrugs
- Lower back stretching
- Ankles and legs stretching

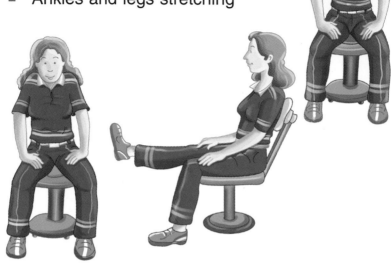

- Massaging tense muscles
- Walking between the tables or along the corridor as much as possible.

Positive Thinking: Think honestly, positively and specifically.

Laughter: Enjoy a good laugh by recollecting some humorous incident in your life.

Self-distraction: During long and heavy working hours, de-stress yourself by standing near a window or sipping a glass of water. You can also do a few stretching exercises while sitting. This will help break the monotony.

Mental Imagery: Relax by thinking about good things (like a future vacation). Lower the noise level around you.

Medication

Proper diet, exercise and a change in lifestyle can reduce cholesterol, but your doctor may advise medication too.

The decision to give you drugs will be based upon the type of hyperlipidaemia you have.

For example:

- High cholesterol with low HDL
- High cholesterol with high LDL
- High cholesterol with high triglycerides
- High triglycerides with low HDL

Medication advised could contain:

- Statins
- Fibrates
- Gemfibrizole
- Niacin
- Ezetimibe
- Any other or combinations of the above

Statins (Atorvastatin, Simvastatin, Pravastatin, Rosuvastatin) are HMG CoA Reductase Inhibitors. They act by blocking the cholesterol synthesis through competitive inhibition in the liver.

The rule of 60

- <60 mg/dl LDL
- >60 mg/dl HDL
- 60% reduction in cardiovascular risk

Do you know that babies do not have atherosclerosis?

Their LDL-C is <50 mg/dl

Cholesterol Absorption Inhibitors

Ezetimibe: It inhibits the absorption of cholesterol selectively. It does not interfere with the absorption of fatty acids and fat soluble vitamins.

Nicotinic Acid Derivatives: They help lower both triglycerides and cholesterol plasma levels. They also aid in increasing the levels of HDL-C.

Omega 3 fish oils: They help reduce levels of cholesterol and triglycerides in plasma.

Fenofibrate: They help lower triglycerides. 15% of cholesterol is only decreased by this medication.

Bezafibrate: It helps suppress endogenous cholesterol synthesis, helping increase specific LDL receptors, which leads to increase in LDL catabolism. It helps increase HDL-C.

Gemfibrizole: It is seen to reduce levels of triglyceride, cholesterol and LDL-C. It also helps increase HDL-C.

Depending upon the individual patient, lipid-lowering drugs can have side effects. There should be no self-medication, a doctor must always be consulted.

Myths and Fact File

Myth

Total cholesterol level below 240 mg/dl is acceptable.

Fact

Total cholesterol should be below 200 mg/dl. LDL (bad cholesterol) must be below 130 mg/dl. If you suffer from heart disease or diabetes, LDL should be below 100 mg/dl. Also, if your HDL (good cholesterol) is below 40 mg/dl, it raises your risk of heart disease.

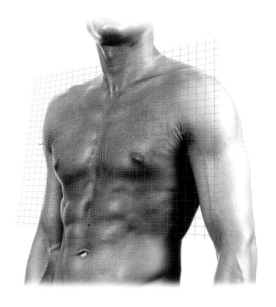

Myth

Vegetable oils are good for the heart.

Fact

All vegetable oils may not be heart-friendly. Palm and coconut oils are high in saturated fat and can raise cholesterol. 'Trans-fats', the partially hydrogenated vegetable oils found in baked foods and margarine, are also known to raise cholesterol.

Vegetable oils like olive, canola and mustard contain mainly monounsaturated and polyunsaturated fats and are good in recommended amounts.

Myth

Good cholesterol (HDL) can only be raised by certain medication.

Fact

Good cholesterol (HDL) can be raised by exercising (about half an hour daily), giving up smoking and losing weight. Medication is recommended if, even after practising the above, the HDL is still low.

High cholesterol need not be a curse. Careful diet management, proper exercise and a regulated lifestyle can help lower cholesterol to acceptable levels so that you can lead a fulfilling life.